Apprentice on a Journey

APPRENTICE ON A JOURNEY

Cover photo
taken in Pakistan by Colin MacLennan
Used by permission.
Cover design by Kent Grey-Hesselbein,
KGB Design Studio
Manchester, TN, USA
http://kghdesign.nvaazion.com/

APPRENTICE ON A JOURNEY

Susan Flemming

APPRENTICE ON A JOURNEY

© 2010 by Susan Flemming,
St. Clair Publications

All rights reserved. No part of this publication may be reproduced or transmitted in any form by any means electronic or mechanical, including telecopy, recording, or any information storage and retrieval system now known or invented, without permission in writing from the publisher, except by a reviewer who wishes to quote brief passages in connection with a review written for inclusion in a magazine, newspaper or broadcast.

ISBN 978-0-9801704-4-3

Printed in the United States of America by
St. Clair Publications
P. O. Box 726
Mc Minnville, TN 37111-0726

http://stan.stclair.net

APPRENTICE ON A JOURNEY

For my son, Colin Arthur MacLennan,
who caught the tears that fell
and dared me on.

APPRENTICE ON A JOURNEY

CONTENTS

Publisher's Introduction	10
About the Author	11
Acknowledgements	12
Renewal	13
Kindness	14
Dylan Thomas at Breakfast	15
Doctor Clock	16
Still Bearing Visions	17
Litany	18
Poem for Mother	19
What the Poet Does	20
Lone Traveler	21
Sonnet	22
Untitled	23
Meditation	24
Potter	25
Marsh Song	26
Untitled	27
Morning Air	28
The Ache in the Heart of it	29
Anguish	30

APPRENTICE ON A JOURNEY

Alone	31
Archeology for Beginners	32
The Girl at Sixteen	33
What is it to be in the Presence of the Beautiful?	34
Sudden as Breath	35
Dissolution	36
Fragments I, II, III, IV	37
V	38
Hillcrest Manors	39
Letter to Madame Roland	40
Tongue in Cheek	41
Ancestor Poem	42
Prayer for Doctor David Baker	43
Prey	44
The Teacher	45
The Rite	46
Croon for Colin	47
Canticle for Colin	48
Poem for my Father	49
Creed	50
Since We Are in Truth Flowers	51
The Curse	52
Gaia	53

APPRENTICE ON A JOURNEY

A Poem for Neil	54
At Forty Below the Mind is Summer	55
Journey	56
Eros Winging	57
Promise	58
The Mind Will Dance	59
Torn Poem	60
To My Friend	61
For Papa	62
Speaking to the Animal Inside	63
For Woman Her Jail	64
Break up Poem	65
The Space Ahead	66
Exchange	67
Nowhere Black	68
Untitled	68
Ocean Mood	69
Whale Moon Light	70
Primordial	71
Untitled	72
An Artist in Disguise Intrigues Me	73
Search	74

APPRENTICE ON A JOURNEY

Untitled	75
Warning	76
Permission to Proceed	77
A Day	78
Bone Picking	79
Lines to Feed the Living	80
Winter Rune	81
Something Lasting Propels Us to the Rim of Our Being	82

APPRENTICE ON A JOURNEY

PUBLISHER'S INTRODUCTION

I had the honor of meeting Susan Flemming in August, 2008 in Halifax, Nova Scotia, Canada, where I was involved as a member of the Executive Committee for the Atlantic Conference, a symposium aimed at presenting evidence of pre-Columbian Atlantic crossings to the New World. The conference featured top experts in the fields of archaeology, linguistics and DNA.

Susan was attending as a reporter / observer. It was my great privilege to be able to spend time with her, on occasion, during the three days I was there. She mentioned the fact that she was a music major and teacher, and had been composing poetical verse for many years, but had never ventured to publish a volume of her work. Being a poet myself, I asked her to send me selections of her poems, and suggested that, based on her merit, I might be interested in publishing it. Upon receiving an email of three of her recent poems, I was blown away by the quality and depth which it reflected.

Among all of the aspiring poets which I have met, I have found none with more originality and talent than she. It is my great pleasure to introduce her outstanding verse to the world in this first small collection. Those who appreciate outstanding talent will, no doubt, drink in her lines, and find themselves, like myself, begging for more. And more there shall be.

Stanley J. "Stan" St. Clair, publisher and editor.

APPRENTICE ON A JOURNEY

ABOUT THE AUTHOR

Susan Flemming was born on January 17, 1956, in Amherst, Nova Scotia, into a family of gifted artists and musicians. Susan stated, "I learned everything I needed to know before I went to school, and never recall learning to read. Somehow I imbibed enough poetry to string a few words together".

Poems included in this volume which were previously published in *Particles*, 1982, Tech Press, Halifax, NS are: Primordial, Ocean Mood, To My Friend, Prey, Letter to Madame Roland, Archeology for Beginners and Creed.

This book represents her early work.

.

APPRENTICE ON A JOURNEY

ACKNOWLEDGEMENTS

The following people have helped me in making this book. Some I have honored by writing poems for them.

James Maclennan
Colin Maclennan
David Francis
Dr. David Baker
the late Hugh MacLennan
Annie MacLeod
Anita MacLeod
Philip McShane
Barry Campbell
Dr. Dora Stinson
the late Harry Flemming
Robert Flemming
the late Evelyn Campbell
Neil Campbell
Albert Flemming
Joan Elizabeth Chipman
Sean Virgo
the late Robert Jones, psychiaterist
Roberta Savoie
Sarah Jackson
Marc Vautour
John Walsh
Dr. Paul MacIntyre
Dr. Margaret Casey
Dr. and Mrs. Edna Handforth
Nicola Young
Jorie Graham
Alistair MacLeod

Nick Mancuso
the late P. K. Page
Margaret Atwood
Nigel Allen
Joseph MacLeod
David MacDonald
Larry Mintz
Pierre Masse
David Walsh
Danny Beaton
the late Florence Flemming
Fred Popowich
Eric Stackhouse
Irving Layton
Seamus Heaney

Marie MacLellan will go down in history as having the distinction of
barring me from the six branches of the Pictou-Antigonish Regional Library
under the Protection of Property Order
for six months between March 2001-October 2001
against the advice of Police Chief White of Trenton, Nova Scotia.
As of this date, I still haven't been informed as to why I had been barred.

Thanks especially to Sharon MacAlpine for believing in this book.

APPRENTICE ON A JOURNEY

RENEWAL

We are fractured
and renewed
in the same breath.

We are brought back
to what we are
time and time again.

We search
never realizing our center
is where we thought
we could never find it.

We are perched on a horizon
sitting on joy unexpressed.

APPRENTICE ON A JOURNEY

KINDNESS

Once in this existence
we meet with a helper
who rides out the chaos
to fathom our hearts.

With whom we need not speak
in order to be understood,
nor weep openly for him
to know our sadness.

With whom we need not agonize
for him to know our guilt and torment,
nor dramatize ourselves,
for he understands us better than we do.

For he sees us,
and loves us
as we were before the pain.
Unscarred.

APPRENTICE ON A JOURNEY

DYLAN THOMAS AT BREAKFAST

I attempt to read Dylan Thomas at breakfast
while a child hammers a block of wood
and sings," Rudolph the Red-Nosed Reindeer"
in clear soprano.

The pipes are frozen.

I open to a poem,
" was there a time."
I imagine him trying to write
in his little cottage in Wales.

The sea drums near his door-step.
Three children and his wife bawl,
" No food, no food."
The cheque from the benefactress
late that month.

Their faces dark and starved like mine workers.

On this side of the Atlantic,
I'm sunk between these purple hills.
A brook cleaves the dagger woods.
The mother demons have retreated
into the serpent dark.
The sun has winked away the pitted moon.

I will share with daylight, what I carved from sleep.

DOCTOR CLOCK

He talks time
while
ordering the universe
to his plate
with his mind.

APPRENTICE ON A JOURNEY

STILL BEARING VISIONS

Poetry is concerned with the breath.
The part of us connected in the womb
to the universal sea.

Seer, to drag up from the depths of being.
To make known so one can forget.

APPRENTICE ON A JOURNEY

LITANY

The body still hungers
in a bone cage
when the sun crawls down
from the mountain.

Two beasts muscle their desire in a frenzy.

The singing children
follow the old drunkard
into the street
to beg for pennies.

We all beg and many times the skin is shed.

It is all quite new,
the sound of flesh
rubbing flesh
and being eaten.

We arise a whole animal pasturing the soul.

APPRENTICE ON A JOURNEY

POEM FOR MY MOTHER

You took a tiny animal
and stretched its skin
on barren tundra
where flowers erupt
like violent secrets held in the earth too long.

You pared down the skin
until it was thin
and almost translucent.
Your fingertips stayed in the parchment.
Four stakes you inserted.
Guilt, anger, despair and hope
you named the corners.

Under the omnipresent Arctic sun
the corner marked hope became brittle
and fluttered away wildly.

The skin of this fragile animal
who is also your daughter
can never release its comfort.

She can never heal your self

APPRENTICE ON A JOURNEY

WHAT THE POET DOES

She is trying to carve with language
to liberate herself from stone.
As Michelangelo's slave emerges
half-formed from marble.
A lump of marble honed from chaos.

Aloneness is her beginning;
a trigger for life.
As she struggles to appease her torment
and make the darkness sing.

APPRENTICE ON A JOURNEY

LONE TRAVELER

I was a lone traveler treading through the dark
when your eyes beckoned
with the power of their light.

A sense of belonging, of country
filled me and I became a child again,
strolling on the fecund earth
alive with humming sounds.

Then, you reached out your arms
to grapple me safe
in the garden of your heart.

APPRENTICE ON A JOURNEY

SONNET

The poet takes us inward to the heart
and breathes a plainsong on this noisy world.
A woman born to mouth the art
that comes to her from outer spheres unfurled.
The rings that gird her in ephemeral thought
ensnare her in a universal bind.
When words inspire, the lines are taut
that join us with a prescient mind.
As we evolve in constant interplay,
not poets we, nor cosmic messengers:
unseeing people, we may lose our way.
Avoiding strife, become its harbinger.

The turmoil of this world has made her keen
to be the eyes for those who have not seen.

UNTITLED

You released me.
It was your thunder,
your storms.
Senses caressed,
mind redressed,
soul reborn.

MEDITATION

I look from the doorway
and see the living trees.
They are breathing,
and so am I.
They have counted
the season's sap in their roots.
The sun has burnished
their leaves and drawn the juice
up from the ground.

They struggle between each other
for the best place in the light.

Leaves arranged like feathers,
Open, close, ready for flight.

APPRENTICE ON A JOURNEY

POTTER

Minerals from the earth
make us what we are.
I can see you sitting
with the elements.
Your hands
reach out,
infused with mind.
On the wheel, strange alchemist visions
come true as a vessel for your thought
turns to stone.

APPRENTICE ON A JOURNEY

MARSH SONG

The sea is held in a huge basin until overflowing,
soaking fringes of turf with finger rivers.
All day organic wastes belch and swell
fertile mulch of sea-bird haven.

The chirr of insects, the fish beating in with the tide.
Shell animals burrow in with thick mud.
Generations that spawn here, die here.

All night mist glides in, quiet and wet.
Shielding creatures in their deep, static pulse of sleep.

UNTITLED

Senescent spirits cloak; they have spoken.
Though ears are still and lips lie dumb,
The earth is moiled with hidden music.
I hear their plaints and suspire.

APPRENTICE ON A JOURNEY

MORNING AIR

Cold jams the knuckles.
A dog yelps in a truck
speeding through the city's yawn.
Bird song thrills.

Morning air
seethes into cells,
fresh as love.

APPRENTICE ON A JOURNEY

THE ACHE IN THE HEART OF IT

The ache in the heart of it.
Creator hear me.
The rooted tree, help it grow.

The earth and her creatures
protect their home.

Help us in our need.
The time is short
to protect the earth
for her children.

Save us, O Creator,
from ourselves.
Always from ourselves.
I taste the ocean's salt
in the tears
flowing from my eyes.

Help us see,
help us see,
help us see

the way through.

ANGUISH

A table was set
for guilt
and she came
and ate.

The meal was a human heart.
Guilt was hungry.

The food was never enough.

APPRENTICE ON A JOURNEY

ALONE

We were traveling on a road
in Cape Breton.
We passed a figure
to the right carrying
a bag of groceries.

Josie stopped the car
and she climbed
onto the back seat.
She clutched the bag
to her lap as if to rock a baby.
Mouth awry and too afraid to speak.

I knew already that
her road would not end
on a well-lit door step
peopled with kindly faces
and merry eyes.

She was a ten-year old
with hair like unwashed feathers
and hollow bones
that could never support the weight
of alcoholic parents.

APPRENTICE ON A JOURNEY

ARCHELOOGY FOR BEGINNERS

Clearly,
I am speaking in degrees.
Egyptian hieroglyphics.
Your art, raised beyond
a certain level.
Eyes from a cave
piercing darkness.
I appear on a line:
Could be horizontal,
does not indicate
speed of light.

All right,
wither before me.
This is not the time of year
for serious pleasure.
Pretend for once
we allow the ultimate deliverance:
safety from the steel trap
- serrated edge – of guilt
closing in on itself.
I will touch you again and again.

APPRENTICE ON A JOURNEY

THE GIRL AT SIXTEEN

The poetry muse takes hold
and pulses like a tiny wing
in her heart.

The silence between beats
is suffocating.
She is riddled with anxiety.
Quivering towards her God.

APPRENTICE ON A JOURNEY

WHAT IS IT TO BE IN THE PRESENCE OF THE BEAUTIFUL?

I do not know the gentle fury
that kindled the light
behind your eyes.
Or why as you walk
the earth opens to receive
her vibrant, loving god-soul,
his voice quaked with laughter.
My bones still ache
a strange music of despair,
and O, when I am with you
how my senses dance.

APPRENTICE ON A JOURNEY

SUDDEN AS BREATH

Sudden as breath,
trust surrounds us
like a skin.

I have known you
when the veins were frozen.
The pathway where you stood eroded.

I don't need to go on foot,
only mind will take me there,
into your eyes where the memory
of a race dwells in the moods
of your face.

DISSOLUTION

With you
I have discovered the distance
between stars.
I do not know
if the neverness of night
can lead us when your eyes view
the long journey ahead.

Or if we will ever ignite
the charred memory
of our embrace.

APPRENTICE ON A JOURNEY

FRAGMENTS

I

Hearing each other
we are drawn into a fold
as sheep needing comfort
and wait separate to dance.

II

To love
meaning goddess
fallen over and over.
Bellies and thighs
mingle into one sound
while I may be new.

III

No special animals,
we embrace
in nocturnal silence.
Night falls
and we sleep,
unaware of the other's breathing
to our own.

IV

Oh love,
I found you:
You my leaf
and I your wind,
unthinking we follow.

APPRENTICE ON A JOURNEY

V

Enveloped
in time
that burns
between our hearts.
Distance and closeness
are the same thing.
The voice and the song.
The sound and the ear.
The memory of you
banishes the distance between us.

APPRENTICE ON A JOURNEY

HILLCREST MANORS

Their bodies have collapsed
like broken bags into wheelchairs.
The nerves spill out.
Animals corralled together
with no sense of direction.
They have come here to wait.
Relatives visit twice a year.
Christmas is spent with a nurse.
Comfort is a bed brought from home.
Convenience is a husband sleeping down the hall.
A nurse whispers in my ear,
"Last year the flu swept through here
and five died in one week.
We call them guests instead of patients
to make them feel more at home".

We forget the furious music
that rippled from palm to palm
and in their dying we shed no light.

APPRENTICE ON A JOURNEY

LETTER TO MADAME ROLAND

Beheaded during the French Revolution.
At the foot of the scaffold she asked for pen and paper
to write down the strange thoughts that were rising in her.
The request was refused.

I squeeze out poems as a bee makes wax
in tiny glands between the creases of her body.
We are thrust into this world and lie between the folds of life.
Death, recoils the mind. Madame, how you knew.
You faced that incubus with your pen. Its ink the elixir.

Although, your request was refused, they could not sever
the spirit from your palm. I built a scaffold for my mind.
Daily, I commence the climb
and am so afraid of being abandoned there.

APPRENTICE ON A JOURNEY

TONGUE IN CHEEK

Old men are friendly,
any woman their goddess.

Old men are wise.
They winnow your thoughts
in their sleep.

Old men are honest.
They carve from your sleep
an escape route for day.

Old men are passionate.
Your body is clay
in their tired hands.

ANCESTOR POEM

It is spring
and the fields
lie brown and moist in winter's rot.

A warm haze climbs the trunks
of the elms by the River.

A man positions himself
on this landscape.

He clings to the soil
that holds
the gnarled bones
of his ancestors.

The scars of living bleed on
and we rage in our hunger
while the little seed
that seeks the soul in us is lost.

APPRENTICE ON A JOURNEY

PRAYER FOR DOCTOR DAVID BAKER

If I could unlock the door to my heart, I could find the key to the world.

People
like little birds
flock to you.

One came dragging
a broken wing.
A sparrow shot down.

We cannot always escape
the danger in this world
yet must live
and seek a sanctuary.

A spirit world inhabits all
if we make room.
Somehow you do.

Your face juts
from the crowd
jolting us with caring.

We seek you
for a landmark
as birds
on a migratory flight
search the same places:

year after year.

Where to nest,
when to rest;
knowing it's alright to come home.

PREY

My body was a house
you flew into,
lodging in the attic
of my thoughts.
Seeking to dwell in your daughter,
unable to live in yourself.

First you swooped to the heart room,
plucking fiber for your nest.
Each time I looked you were there,
nesting in the rafters,
threatening to topple the beams.

I retreated to the root cellar
to learn the axiom of rebirth.

In my garden I built a house for you.
Boarded up the windows except for one.

At night I hear you flail against it,
trying to shatter the glass.

APPRENTICE ON A JOURNEY

THE TEACHER

I asked you about electricity at six,
current flowing,
light flickering.
What did it mean?
"You wouldn't understand that now.
Ask me when you are older."
The connection faltered.

APPRENTICE ON A JOURNEY

THE RITE   for Jorie Graham

I am prompted to write
as a bird is tempted to sing
when the air hits its throat.
Once as a child, I saw the skin under a swallow's beak pulsing:
translucent, veined as a baby's fontanelle.

The last step before sound.

APPRENTICE ON A JOURNEY

CROON FOR COLIN

Little fountains of trust
spring up with you, my child,
opening windows to secret domes.
You look past the world,
are its future, and O, what a blessing, a blessing.
O God, his breath pulses
like a tiny fish.
Phantom spirit,
trusting elf.
Little moon eyes drunk on my milk.

APPRENTICE ON A JOURNEY

CANTICLE FOR COLIN

Darling,
one night
you blew in
on a gale wind.

The windowless room
greeted you,
bold visitor from the netherworld.
Sea visions engulfed
your wild and groping eyes.

Now as you sleep,
the raucous lull
of your breath is comfort
like waves breaking on a beach.

O child, you hold me to this life.

APPRENTICE ON A JOURNEY

POEM FOR MY FATHER

"Real poetry comes out helplessly in spite of silence" - Seamus Heaney

You peopled our home
with everyone you loved.
Mozart, Beethoven, and Vivaldi.
Shakespeare, Blake and Yeats.
You quoted Robbie Burns
at the dinner table.

Behind the house grew
a wild pear tree.
One year it bore boxes of fruit.
The next year, none.

We had to tear away the vine
that snaggled our feet
in the undergrowth,
and threatened to choke the tree.

You showed us the wee eggs
of the hummingbird
in the honeysuckle bush,
the nuthatch nestled
in the spruce bough
and the mating flight
of the queen bee.

Harbored briefly,
in the tidal water at dusk
I bare my senses to the world.

Although my cries were muted
Before they reached my throat,
still I speak to you
in unbroken utterance.

CREED

Poetry is something
I haul up from the gut.
I would rather have nothing
to do with it.
I am the mother.
Some I have to free
like the one that was born
with the cord around its neck.

APPRENTICE ON A JOURNEY

SINCE WE ARE IN TRUTH FLOWERS

I think we were born
a second time.
because the first,
hazardous, unplanned
does not prepare us
for the shock of awakening.
You must be beauty,
for the long fingers
of your love
hook even despair.

APPRENTICE ON A JOURNEY

THE CURSE

My mind cannot escape the curse
of your absence.
I hawk a path across the sky,
my senses eared for clues.
Where last you walked
in a feathered coat
slipping through the grasses.
I am left pondering the traces,
tracking relentlessly across the sky.

APPRENTICE ON A JOURNEY

GAIA

I see her in the mountains.
She is tree-flowering, stream gushing
over roots that seek and open.

Her scent has brushed me
and I dart after her
like a mad swallow.

I watch her dig a hole
to land her babies in.

And speaking runes
to the little ones,
she leads them into her world.

APPRENTICE ON A JOURNEY

POEM FOR NEIL

Connections
between stars
keep us coming back to this place.
Your eyes, their brilliance.

Where were you when
they hurled the placenta
into the ordered dark?
So much past underground:
buried.

I saw a man outside the glassed-in nursery
pointing to his daughter,
"That's her!"

APPRENTICE ON A JOURNEY

AT FORTY BELOW THE MIND IS SUMMER

I am not aware of missing anything.
Each moment seems so right.

The voices crying "should do"
have stopped.

Even your cries have become riderless,
galloping toward sleep.

The backbone stiffens.
A flower stalk strains in the wind.

Another catechism
thrown on the fire.

JOURNEY

I wander down pathways
of hidden and unseen grief.
Is this the slow death
of what we all represent?

I ache to move to some place clear,
past the muddied silt-land.

A river snakes past the dagger woods,
its water dark and rippling.

I long to follow that mysterious path
down to the ocean.

APPRENTICE ON A JOURNEY

EROS WINGING

I am your body's naked apprentice.
How fluid that sense of dive.
I seldom need that dam of fear
that sunk me straight to uncharted waters – stone.

APPRENTICE ON A JOURNEY

PROMISE

It is getting dark
and you have only
so many days
before this life is gone:
your light is taken.
Then surely,
the hand that reached out
has joined you
with this world.

APPRENTICE ON A JOURNEY

THE MIND WILL DANCE

Which came first,
the rhythm or the word?
The spine cushions the mind.

Fresh heaves against the collar bone.

Hands, final carvers, expand the dark.

APPRENTICE ON A JOURNEY

TORN POEM

Out there,
on the wild prairie,
I met an Asian immigrant
in a bar.
He could not stop wringing his hands
long enough to shake mine.
The past trails behind him
like a torn net.
He alone survived the crossing.
A fellow from the unemployment center
found him a job painting
empty ceramic vessels.

APPRENTICE ON A JOURNEY

TO MY FRIEND

After all,
they said you had the disease,
you, a phoenix,
rising.
We all succumb
and seem strangely jealous
of one pretending nothing,
even taking delight in rare
flights of mind.
This world is not livable
except for a few
who organize the nest.
Let the mind stay gristled,
tough, hard to chew.
Let them choke trying
to digest you.

APPRENTICE ON A JOURNEY

FOR PAPA

When I was a little girl
you didn't live
in our house.
Your spirit ran ragged
over the country
and hid in the woods.

Our mother became frantic
when you left.
I just watched.
Now, as I write about you,
it's a weird kind of revenge.

APPRENTICE ON A JOURNEY

SPEAKING TO THE ANIMAL INSIDE

The day shrivels
in front of me
until I cannot see.

A fish bone is stuck
in my throat.
My skin is scales
lying the wrong way
on flesh no one can touch.

This rage is all
and fills me.
A blood I cannot drink from:
it will not nourish.

Longing and loathing
are twin panthers
that circle my bed each night.

"Lie down, lie down," I say, "and sleep."

APPRENTICE ON A JOURNEY

FOR WOMAN HER JAIL

This is a crude attempt to understand.
I know you spent your girlhood in hiding.
An alien, yet you were, when that doctor
imprisoned you. He sealed the lid.
Gave his permission. Said, "Alright, you hide."

Why did you let him bring you out
with crude shocks and new treatments?
He was the jailer. He had your key.
He blustered in, breaking down the soul's door.

He replaced it haphazardly,
so it will not open
and cannot close.
Now it just flails on one weakening hinge.

When I think of you,
I imagine the sea
roiling an underwater world
we know so little about.

I shudder when I think
you cannot rear up for reprisal.
And now you say your destroyer needs you.
You led from the throat. He takes his place in you.

You struggle, yet you cannot move him.
He has taken the shape of you
and lives year-round:
ice frozen in your cup.

APPRENTICE ON A JOURNEY

BREAKUP POEM

It's all over now.
I had to leave.
The first poem I wrote
I crumpled in my hands.
A hellish statement
so truthful it seemed odd.

You stood there
and the pain shot from your eyes
like a machine-gun fire.
The pain I came to know and couldn't bear.
The deep yolk of relation splintered
and we stand apart now.

Two mountains buffeting an icy wind.

APPRENTICE ON A JOURNEY

THE SPACE AHEAD

We have come down from the mountain.
In the hollow of my body,
our baby lived, sucking on the juices,
growing strong. I have lain
in the curve of your back
while my hands licked
the honeyed warmth in your skin.

I have loved the length
of your smooth thighs.
The breadth you gave, I realize,
now you are gone.

APPRENTICE ON A JOURNEY

EXCHANGE

In the winter he took a hostage
and she ransomed her desire.
A body warm,
impressionable as a handful of raw earth,
he sank into her.
All through the long months of cold, she grew.
She watered the seed of want,
but she buried the root of need.

APPRENTICE ON A JOURNEY

NOWHERE BLACK

The cauldron of night is empty
except for the stars.
Pinnacles of light
stuck in space
where we alone
are fathomless.

UNTITLED

Look at the rocks by the edge of the ocean
and see the warning written there.
The way they were thrown,
the pattern they make.

The people are seeking with a sickening haste.
Everything is available.

OCEAN MOOD

Gloom outside. Rained all night.
The cold season of rain.
In the bones a narrow filament
reaches inward and leeches out strength.
Fortitude disappears
in the season of damp wind.
It blows you sideways on the street
and needles the flesh on your face.
This cold season when even birds
swallow their notes
and trees with patchwork leaves
design themselves into the ground
where roots clutch the earth to steady.

APPRENTICE ON A JOURNEY

WHALE MOON NIGHT

Here near the edge,
before we dissolve
into the sea
were creatures like us
who decided to lunge,
and we stayed to grasp
the crumbling land.

So we meet sometimes
in warm flesh havens.
An animal wiser than us
sings through water and bone.

Meanwhile,
the moon holds us
in her dispassionate eye
when we become vicious
and turn on ourselves
like unmothered children.

APPRENTICE ON A JOURNEY

PRIMORDIAL

Before birth
a strange sea molds us.
The beast that crawls out
contains an ocean element.
Later,
standing near the edge,
we watch the shore submit
to roar and rage.
The undertow our conscience.

UNTITLED

Their meeting
was a breath exchanged
beyond the will.

They sat
with the sea.

The moon
had pinned her
to its revolving wheel.
Their subtle looks
would rearrange the night.

APPRENTICE ON A JOURNEY

AN ARTIST IN DISGUISE INTRIGUES ME

I carve
transparent images
which you perceive behind
the safety of your mask:
any painted face will do.

I mastermind
nascent chimeras
while writing runes
naked to the world.

Ask me,
and I'll tell you
screaming on paper
is far better than hiding
behind silence
ruptured by storms.

APPRENTICE ON A JOURNEY

SEARCH

The mind is a wilderness made habitable by poetry.

We have taken the woman
and set her upon the forest floor
buried in moss, needles, seeds and twigs.

The rings of the tree
start with spiraled, inmost circle.
The core will rot.

How soon the strangling legacy
of the dead returns.

Surrendered like this for generations,
she awakens to a search.

Old torments drone in the underbush.
Branches flap like slamming doors.
A river snakes bone-black to the sea.

Once she starts on the path,
there is no turning back.

APPRENTICE ON A JOURNEY

UNTITLED

I hear music
in the heart
that beats under your pain.

I have carried your medicine
for fifty-two moons.

I have waited long
for a break
in this stillness:
for a sign in the night sky.

This morning,
as the sun glinted across
the eastern sky
I heard a song
from the bird of belonging

who only wants
to fly home.

APPRENTICE ON A JOURNEY

WARNING

Where there is potential for love,
there is room to hurt.
Where there is room for hurt,
anger will spring forth.
Where there is no anger,
you will never find love.

Fear the one who never admits to anger.

APPRENTICE ON A JOURNEY

PERMISSION TO PROCEED

Rocks and a garden
are balanced hopes
when the soil is a comfort,
like a warm cloth against the skin.

Who knows what heals
who won't dig down?

Does faith need a human face?

I trust the secret of the curled leaf
unfolding in its time.

APPRENTICE ON A JOURNEY

A DAY

At noon,
the deep grass
still wet on the stalks
hauls in the sunlight.

At dusk,
when the lush foliage
is quiet one flower
won't close
to make its food.

A swallow,
swift as death darts past
my ear.

A day,
when fear in the world
could make us
stop loving
our children.

APPRENTICE ON A JOURNEY

BONE PICKING

" Immortality," she said.
" Yes, tell me what it is," she said.
" Men want to find a substitute for death," she said.
" Let me be immortal so I will never die," he said.
" As if a man could choose," she said.
" A man can choose what he is while he lives," he said.
" Others decide about him when he is gone," she said.

APPRENTICE ON A JOURNEY

LINES TO FEED THE LIVING

Lately,
it has been a day
of disturbance,
cloistered in the shadows
that hold your face
moving tenderly
towards an apex of star.

With you,
time passes more slowly
caught
in the web of embrace
following the winds of impulsiveness
tapped at the peak of creation.

Of everything that is left:
only one explanation I make.
We fear dominance,
we fear dominance
and thereby heed it.

Height and depth,
being and nothingness
is all the same thing.

We don't go anywhere except back into the earth.
There is nothing to be immortal for.

APPRENTICE ON A JOURNEY

WATER RUNE   for Sean

The last place you left, love, gull-ridden
littered with hungry cries.
Pinned between two rocks
a flower grew. Its roots fasted
on the stone.

Your eyes cast live
into still waters
where fish swim up
mouths gaping.
All the creatures
I don't want to live
are still behind my eyes.

Even the ones with their throats cut,
so they cannot sing;
rise up and begin a dance for you.

Although I grasp you are not there.
You lurch in the seaweed's tangled hair.
Your scent leaches through wary flesh.
You fletched me in the minnow's stream.

I wasn't your creature until then.

APPRENTICE ON A JOURNEY

SOMETHING LASTING PROPELLS US TO THE RIM OF OUR BEING

Suddenly I know that beyond logic
I am writing what was predestined to be written,
as long ago I enacted
what I was destined to become.
As seers we grope,
always on the fringe of our failings.

www.ingramcontent.com/pod-product-compliance
Lightning Source LLC
Chambersburg PA
CBHW071330040426
42444CB00009B/2121